WE ARE A FAMILY
Tell the Kid about Adoption and make them feel equally loved

To answer this question we will tell the story of the Robertson family and the day they decided to adopt a kid.

Six years ago, the Robertson family...

...composed of Marilyn, a very nice and funny woman...

...and Marlon, a reserved and admirable man.

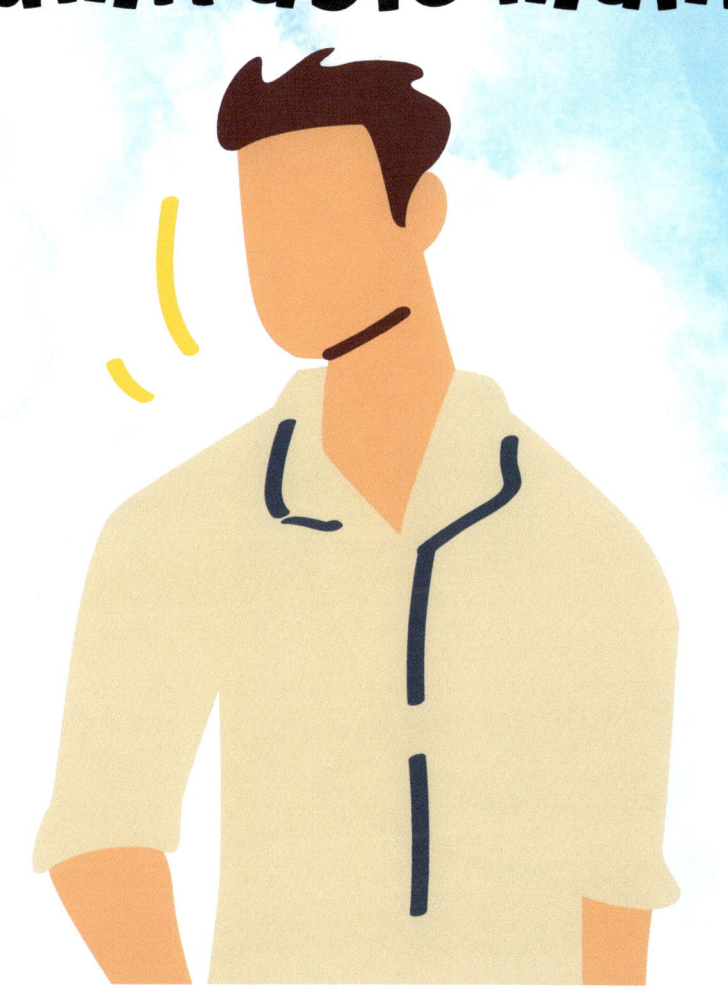

After two years of marriage...

Unfortunately though, things don't always go as planned and something magical can always happen that can radically change someone's life.

Ms. Marilyn, despite her young age, is unable to have babies due to a health problem.

She longed so much to have a baby of her own....

...but, nevertheless, she understands something special.

She understands that her love to offer unconditionally will be able to give it to a kid she will love with all her heart.

Together with her husband Marlon, they decide that if they're not going to be "belly parents,"...

In the magical place where the kids are adopted, they find Jack: a little boy with two big eyes and a smile who immediately makes Mrs. Marilyn and her husband Marlon fall in love.

So Jack from that special day became a member and an integral part of the Robertson family!

Anyone who is loved unconditionally by someone.....

...regardless of gender...

...by blood ties or skin color....

...will always be part of a family.

For it is love that makes us part of something great.

Printed in Great Britain
by Amazon